THE COLLECTED WRITINGS OF
OF
JACK PARSONS

THE BOOK OF BABALON
THE BOOK OF ANTICHRIST
ANALYSIS BY A MASTER OF THE TEMPLE

AF398027

© 2023 Culturea Editions
Texte et illustration de couverture : © domaine public
Edition : Culturea (Hérault, 34)
Contact : infos@culturea.fr
Retrouvez notre catalogue sur http://culturea.fr
Imprimé en Allemagne par Books on Demand
Design typographique : Derek Murphy
Layout : Reedsy (https://reedsy.com/)
Dépôt légal : janvier 2023
Tous droits réservés pour tous pays
ISBN : 9791041942831

CONTENTS

The Book Of Babalon

The Book Of Antichrist

Analysis By A Master Of The Temple

TheBookOfBabalon

January4-Mar ch4,1946E. V.

INTRODUCTION

This book contains the record of a magical experiment relating to the invocation of an elemental, the thereafter of the Goddess or Force called BABALON, and the results thereof. An appendix con- tains some details of the method, published for the first time. The contents should be clear enough to those who are prepared for understanding, and a little study and effort should make it so for those who desire understanding. For the rest, each will no doubt interpret it in accord with his own predilections.

A note on the underlying philosophy. The present age is under the influence of the force called, in magical terminology, Horus. This force relates to fire, Mars, and the sun, that is, to power, violence, and energy. It also relates to a child, being innocent (i.e. undifferentiated). Its manifestations may be noted in the destruction of old institutions and ideas, the discovery and liberation of new energies, and the trend towards power governments, war, homosexuality, infantilism, and schizophrenia.

This force is completely blind, depending upon the men and women in whom it manifests and who guide it. Obviously, its guidance now tends towards catastrophy.

The catastrophic trend is due to our lack of understanding of our own natures. The hidden lusts, fears, and hatreds resulting from the warping of the love urge, which underly the natures of all Western peoples, have taken a homicidal and suicidal direction.

This impasse is broken by the incarnation of another sort of force, called BABALON. The nature of this force relates to love,

understanding, and dionysian freedom, and is the necessary counterbalance or correspondence to the manifestation of Horus.

It is indicated that this force is actually incarnate in some living
woman, as the result of the described magical operation. A more basic
matter, however, is the indication that this force is incarnate in all
men and women, and needs only to be invoked to free the spirit from
the debris of the old aeon, and to direct the blind force of Horus into
constructive channels of under- standing and love. The methods of
this invocation are described in the text.

The background of this material may be found in the Book of the Law,
the Comment thereon, and other writings of Aleister Crowley; also in
various magical, anthropological, psychological, and philosophical
texts. These are all necessary to an understanding and use of the
material.

One further point. It should be remembered that all human activi-
ties, after the vital functions are fulfilled, arise from the need to love
or to be loved. It is therfore quite literally true that in understanding
(i.e. that which embraces all categories of love) is all power given. A
grasp of the principle of bipolarity should make this clear.

With this crude and rudimentary philosophical discourse, then, I
present the Book of Babalon:

A.CONCEPT ION

In January 1946 I had been engaged in the study and practice of
Magick for seven years, and in the supervision and operation of an
occult lodge for four years, having been initiated into the Sanctuary
of the Gnosis by the Beast 666, Fra. 132, and Fra. Saturnus. At this
time I decided upon a Magical operation de- signed to obtain the
assistance of an elemental mate. This is a well known procedure in
Magick (cf. Ch. VIII in Magick in Theory and Practice), consisting of

the invocation of a spirit or ele- mental into tangible existence by various magical techniques.

I decided upon the use of the Enochian Tablets obtained by Dr. Dee and Edward Kelley, employing the *n*n*n square of the Air Tablet. The technique was approximately as follows:

(January 4, 1946, 9:00 PM)

1. Prepared and consecrated Air Dagger. (The other magical weapons were previously prepared. This dagger served as the special talisman of the operation.) 2. Prepared Enochian Air Tablet on virgin parchment. 3. Prepared Parchment Talisman 4. Rituals as follows: (a) Invoking Pentagram of Air. (b) Invocation of Bornless One. (c) Conjuration of Air. (d) Consecration of Air Dagger. (e) Key Call of third Aire. (f) Invocation of God and King of Aire. (g) Invocation of Six Seniors. (h) Invocation of (RZDA) by *n*n*n and (EXARP), to visible ap- pearance. (i) Invocaton of wand with material basis on talisman. (j) Invocation with dagger. (k) License to depart, purification, and banishing. I followed this procedure for eleven days, from January 4 to 15, with the following entries in my record: January 5. A strong windstorm beginning suddenly about the middle of the first invocation. Jan 6. Invoked as before. Wind storm continued intermittently all day and night. Jan 7. Invoked twice. Wind subsided. Used Prokofief Violin Con- certo No. 2 as musical background. Jan 8. Invoked twice, using blood. Jan 9. Invoked twice, replenishing material basis. Jan 10. Invoked twice. I retired about 11 PM, and was awakened at 12 PM by nine strong, rapid knocks. A table lamp at the opposite corner of the room was thrown violently to the floor and broken. There was no window in this corner, and no wind was blowing at the time.

(Note. I have had little experience with phenomena of this sort. Magically speaking, it usually represents "breaks" in the opera- tion, indicating imperfect technique. Actually, in any magical opeation there should be no phenomena but the willed result.)

Jan 11. Invoked twice, using blood.

Jan 12. Invoked twice. A heavy windstorm.

Jan 13. Invoked twice. Windstorm continued.

Jan 14. The light system of the house failed about 9 PM. Another magician who had been staying at the house and studying with me, was carrying a candle across the kitchen when he was struck strongly on the right shoulder, and the candle knocked out of his hand. He called us, and we observed a brownish yellow light about seven feet high in the kitchen.

I banished with a magical sword, and it disappeared. His right arm was paralyzed for the rest of the night.

Jan 15. Invoked twice. At this time the Scribe developed some sort of astral vision, describing in detail an old enemy of mine of whom he had never heard, and later the guardian forms of Isis and the Archangel Michael. Later, in my room, I heard the raps again, and a buzzing, metallic voice crying "let me go free." I felt a great pressure and tension in the house that night, which was also noticed by the other occupants. There was no other phenomena, and I admit a feeling of disappointment.

The feeling of tension and unease continued for four days. Then, on January 18, at sunset, while the Scribe and I were on the Mojave desert, the feeling of tension suddenly snapped. I turned to him and said, "it is done," in absolute certainty that the operation was accomplished. I returned home, and found a young woman answering the requirements waiting for me. She is describa- ble as an air of fire type with bronze red hair, fiery and sub- tle, determined and obstinate, sincere and perverse, with ex- traordinary personality, talent, and intelligence.

During the period of January 19 to February 27 I invoked the Goddess BABALON with the aid of my magical partner, as was proper to one of my grade.

B.COMMU NICATIONS

On February 27 my magical partner went East for a visit, and on Feb. 28 I went back to the Mojave, invoking BABALON. During this invocation, the presence of the Goddess came upon me, and I was commanded to write the following communication:

LIBER 49

1. Yea, it is I, BABALON.

2. And this is my book, that is the fourth chapter of the Book of the Law, He completing the Name, for I am out of NUIT by HORUS, the incestuous sister of RA-HOOR-KHUIT.

3. It is BABALON. TIME IS. Ye fools.

4. Thou hast called me, oh accursed and beloved fool.

5-8. (Missing and presumed lost. Ed.)

9. Now know that I, BABALON, would take flesh and come among men.

10. I will come as a penelous (sic) flame, as a devious song, a trumpet in judgement halls, a banner before armies.

11. And gather my children unto me, for THE TIME is at hand.

12. And this is the way of my incarnation. Heed!

13. Thou shalt offer all thou art and all thou hast at my altar, witholding nothing. And thou shalt be smitten full sore and thereafter thou shalt be outcast and accursed, a lonely wanderer in abominable places.

14. Ye Dare. I have asked of none other, nor have they asked. Else is vain. But thou hast willed it.

15. Know then that thus I came to thee before, thou a great Lord, and I a maid enrapt. Ah blind folly.

16. And thereafter madness, all in vain. Thus it has been, multi- form. How thou hast burned beyond.

17. I shall come again, in the form thou knowest. Now it shall be thy blood.

18. The altar is aright, and the robe.

19. The perfume is sandal, and the cloth green and gold. There is my cup, our book, and thy dagger.

20. There is a flame.

21. The sigil of devotion. Be it consecrated, be it true, be it daily affirmed. I am not scorned. Thy love is to me. Procure a disk of copper, in diameter three inches paint thereon the field blue the star gold of me, BABALON.

22. It shall be my talisman. Consecrate with the supreme rituals of the word and the cup.

23. My calls as thou knowest. All love songs are of me. Also seek me in the Seventh Aire.

24. This for a time appointed. Seek not the end, I shall instruct thee in my way. But be true. Would it be hard if I were thy lover, and before thee? But I am thy lover and I am with thee.

25. I shall provide a vessel, when or whence I say not. Seek her not, call her not. Let her declare. Ask nothing. Keep silence. There shall be ordeals.

26. My vessel must be perfect. This is the way of her perfection.

27. The working is of nine moons.

28. The Astarte working, with music and feasting, with wine and all arts of love.

29. Let her be dedicated, consecrated, blood to blood, heart to heart, mind to mind, single in will, none without the circle, all to me.

30. And she shall wander in the witchwood under the Night of Pan, and know the mysteries of the Goat and the Serpent, and of the children that are hidden away.

31. I will provide the place and the material basis, thou the tears and blood.

32. Is it difficult, between matter and spirit? For me it is ecstacy and agony untellable. But I am with thee. I have large strength, have thou likewise.

33. Thou shalt prepare my book for her instruction, also thou shalt teach that she may have captains and adepts in her service. Yea, thou shalt take the black pilgrimage, but it will not be thou that returnest.

34. Let her prepare her work according to my voice in her heart, with thy book as guide, and none other instructing.

35. And let her be in all things wise, and sure, and excellent.

36. But let her think on this: my way is not in the solemn ways, or in the reasoned ways, but in the wild free way of the eagle, and the devious way of the serpent, and the oblique way of the factor unknown and unnumbered.

37. For I am BABALON, and she my daughter, unique, and there shall be no other women like her.

38. In My Name shall she have all power, and all men and excel- lent things, and kings and captains and the secret ones at her command.

39. The first servants are chosen in secret, by my force in her--a captain, a lawyer, an agitator, a rebel--I shall provide.

40. Call me, my daughter, and I shall come to thee. Thou shalt be full of my force and fire, my passion and power shall surround and inspire thee; my voice in thee shall judge nations.

41. None shall resist thee, whom I lovest. Though they call thee harlot and whore, shameless, false, evil, these words shall be blood in their mouths, and dust thereafter.

42. But my children will know thee and love thee, and this will make them free.

43. All is in thy hands, all power, all hope, all future.

44. One came as a man, and was weak and failed.

45. One came as a woman, and was foolish, and failed.

46. But thou art beyond man and woman, my star is in thee, and thou shalt avail.

47. Even now thy hour strikes upon the clock of my FATHER. For He prepared a banquet and a Bridal Bed. I was that Bride, appointed from the beginning, as it was written T.O.P.A.N.

48. Now is the hour of birth at hand. Now shall my adept be crucified in the Basilisk abode. 49. Thy tears, thy sweat, thy blood, thy semen, thy love, thy faith shall provide. Ah, I shall drain thee like the cup that is of me, BABALON.

50. Stand thou fast, and I shall pass the first veil to speak with thee, through the stars shake. 51. Stand thou fast, and I shall pass the second veil, while God and Jesus be smitten with the sword of HORUS.

52. Stand thou fast, and I shall pass the third veil, and the shapes of hell shall be turned again to loveliness.

53. For thy sake shall I stride through the flames of Hell, though my tongue be bitten through.

54. Let me behold thee naked and lusting after me, calling upon my name.

55. Let me receive all thy manhood within my Cup, climax upon climax, joy upon joy.

56. Yea, we shall conquer death and Hell together.

57. And the earth is mine.

58. Thou shalt (make the?) Black Pilgrimage.

59. Yea it is even I BABALON and I SHALL BE FREE. Thou fool, be

thou also free of sentimentality. Am I thy village queen and thou a sophomore, that thou shouldst have thy nose in my buttocks?

60. It is I, BABALON, ye fools, MY TIME is come, and this my book that my adept prepares is the book of BABALON.

61. Yea, my adept, the Black Pilgrimage. Thou shalt be accursed, and this is the nature of the curse. Thou shalt publish the secret matter of the adepts thou knowest, witholding no word of it, in an appendix to this my Book. So they shall cry fool, liar, sot, traducer, betrayer. Thou art not glad thou meddled with magick?

62. There is no other way, dear fool, it is the eleventh hour.

63. The seal of my Brother is upon the earth, and His Avatar is before you. There is threshing of wheat and a trampling of grapes that shall not cease until the truth be known unto the least of men.

64. But you who do not accept, you who see beyond, reach out your hands my children and reap the world in the hour of your harvest.

65. Gather together in the covens as of old, whose number is eleven, that is also my number. Gather together in public, in song and dance and festival. Gather together in secret, be naked and shameless and rejoice in my name.

66. Work your spells by the mode of my book, practicing secretly, inducing the supreme spell.

67. The work of the image, and the potion and the charm, the work of the spider and the snake, and the little ones that go in the dark, this is your work.

68. Who loves not hates, who hates fears, let him taste fear.

69. This is the way of it, star, star. Burning bright, moon, witch moon.

70. You the secret, the outcast, the accursed and despised, even you that gathered privily of old in my rites under the moon.

71. You the free, the wild, the untamed, that walk now alone and forlorn.

72. Behold, my Brother cracks the world like a nut for your eating.

73. Yea, my Father has made a house for you, and my Mother has prepared a Bridal Bed. My Brother has confounded your enemies.

74. I am the Bride appointed. Come ye to the nuptials--come ye now!

75. My joy is the joy of eternity, and my laughter is the drunken laughter of a harlot in the house of ecstasy.

76. All you loves are sacred, pledge them all to me.

77. Set my star upon your banners and go forward in joy and victory. None shall deny you, and none shall stand before you, because of the Sword of my Brother. Invoke me, call upon me, call me in your convocations and rituals, call upon me in your loves and battles in my name BABALON, wherein is all power given!

C.BI RTH

[March 2, 1946 E.V.]

On March 1 and 2 1946 I prepared the altar and equipment in accordance with the instructions in Liber 49. The Scribe had been away about a week, and knew nothing of my invocations of BABALON, which I had kept entirely secret. On the night of March 2 he returned, and described a vision he had that evening of a savage and beautiful woman riding naked on a great cat-like beast. He was impressed with the urgent necessity of giving me some message or communication. We prepared magically for this communication, constructing a temple at the altar with the analysis of the key word. He was robed in white, carrying the lamp, and I in black, hooded, with the cup and dagger. At his suggestion we played Rachmanninoff's Isle of the Dead as background music, and set an automatic recorder to transcribe any audible occurrences. At approximately 8 PM he began to dictate, I transcribing directly as I received.

THE SCRIBE: "The Angel of TARO. A three day retirement to greet her. Purify thyself. The symbol is seven by three. It is BABALON. Keep secret. The communications are sacred."

"These are the preparations. Green gold cloth, food for the Beast, upon a hidden platter, back of the altar. Disclose only when the doors are bolted."

"Transgression is death."

"Back of main altar. Prepare instantly. Light the first flame at 10 PM, March 2, 1946."

"The year of BABALON is 4063."

"Beware of the use of profaned rituals."

"She is flame of life, power of darkness, she destroys with a glance, she may take thy soul. She feeds upon the death of men."

"Beautiful--Horrible."

The Scribe, now pale and sweating, rested awhile, then continued:

[TheFir stRitual]

"The first ritual. Tomorrow the second ritual. Concentrate all force and being in Our Lady BABALON. Light a single light on Her altar, saying: Flame is Our Lady, flame is Her hair. I am flame."

"A plate of food, unsalted. An altar cloth hitherto undefiled."

"Make a box of blackness at ten o'clock. Smear the vessel which contains flame with thine own blood. Destroy at the altar a thing of value. Remain in perfect silence, and heed the voice of Our Lady. Speak not of this ritual or of Her coming to any person. If asked, answer in a manner that avoids suspicion. Nor speculate at any time as to Her future mortal identity. To receive flatter- ing communications to thy damnation. Press not to receive teach- ings beyond those given."

"Questions: you may ask but three. Spend one half hour in composing these at 11:30 PM. The answers must be written at midnight."

"Thou shalt take the alkahest in thine own mouth, and in the box of darkness carefully store this matter."

"Display thyself to Our Lady; dedicate thy organs to Her, dedi- cate thy heart to Her, dedicate thy mind to Her, dedicate thy soul to Her, for She shall absorb thee, and thou shalt become living flame before She incarnates. For it shall be through you alone, and no one else can help in this endeavour."

"It is lonely, it is awful."

"Retire from human contact until noon tomorrow. Clear all profane documents on the morrow, before receiving further instructions. Consult no book but thine own mind. Thou art a god. Behave at this altar as one god before another. And so be prosperity."

"Thou art the guardian and thou art the guide, thou art the worker and the mechanic. So conduct thyself. Discuss nothing of this matter until thou art certain that thine understanding embraces all."

Here the Scribe ceased dictation. I proceeded to follow these instructions and those of March 1, utilizing the following ritu- als. I include the rituals used in the operation of the first night, in order to indicate the nature of the Force invoked.

1

[TheFir stInv ocation]

The temple is opened with the analysis of the key word:

I N R I. Yod Nun Resh Yod. Virgo Isis Mighty Mother. Scorpio Apophis Destroyer. Sol, Osiris slain and risen. IAO. The sign of Osiris slain (given). The sign of the mourning of Isis (given). The sign of Apophis and Typhon (given). LVX, Lux, the Light of the Cross.

The invoking hexagram is drawn in the four quarters and the name ARARITA vibrated in each quarter. In closing, the hexagram is reversed.

2

The[Se cond]Inv ocation
(FromtheGnosticMass)

THEP RIEST

"O circle of stars whereof our Father is but the younger brother, marvel beyond imagination, soul of infinite space, before whom time is ashamed, the mind bewildered, and the understanding dark, not unto thee may we attain unless thine image be love. Therefore by seed and root and stem and bud and leaf and flower and fruit do we invoke thee."

BABALON

"But to love me is better than all things; if under the night stars in the desert thou presently burnest mine incense before me, invoking me with a pure heart and the serpent flame therein, thou shalt come a little to lie in my bosom. For one kiss wilt thou be willing to give all. But whoso gives one particle of dust shall lose all in that hour. Ye shall gather goods and store of women and spices; ye shall wear rich jewels; ye shall exceed the nations of earth in splendour and pride; but always in the love of me, and so shall ye come to my joy. I charge you earnestly to come before me in a single robe, and covered with a rich head- dress. I love you! I yearn to you! Pale or purple, veiled or voluptuous, I who am all pleasure and purple and drunkenness of the innermost sense, desire you. Put on the wings, and arouse the coiled splendour within you: come unto me! to me! Sing the rap- turous love songs unto me! Burn to me perfume! Drink to me, for I love you! I love you! I am the blue lidded daughter of sunset, I am the naked brilliance of the voluptuous night sky. To me. To me."

3

TheThir dInv ocation.

(FromTheVisionandtheV   oice)

CHORUS

"Glory unto the Scarlet Woman, BABALON, the Mother of Abomina-
tion, that rideth upon the Beast, for She hath spilt their blood in every
corner of the earth, and lo! She hath mingled it in the cup of Her
whoredom."

"With the breath of Her kisses hath she fermented it, and it hath
become the wine of the Sabbath; and in the Holy Assembly hath She
poured it out for Her worshippers; and they have become drunken
thereon, so that face to face they beheld my Father. Thus are they
made worthy to partake of the mystery of this holy vessel, for the
blood is the life."

"Beautiful art thou O BABALON, and desirable, for thou hast given
Thyself to everything that liveth, and thy weakness hath subdued
their strength. For in that union Thou didst understand. There- fore
art Thou called Understanding, O BABALON, Lady of the Night."

"O my God, in one last rapture let me attain to the union of the one
with the many. For She is Love, and Her Love is one, and She has
divided theone love into infinite loves, and each love is one, and equal
with the One, and therefore is She passed from the Assembly and the
Law and the enlightenment into the anarchy of solitude and darkness.
For ever thus must She veil the brilliance of Herself."

4

[TheFourthInv ocation]

O BABALON, BABALON beloved, come now, partake of the
sacrament, possess this shrine. Take me now! Let me be drunken on

the wine of your fornications; let your kisses wanton me to death. Accept thou this sacrifice willingly given!

5

TheFifthInv ocation
TheCalloftheSe venthAir e

Rass I Salman Paradiz Oa-Crimi Aao Ial-Pir-Gah Qui-In Enay Butmon Od I Noas Ni Paradial Casarmg Vgear Chirlan Od Zonac Luciftan Cors Ta Vaul Zirn Tol Hami Sobol Ondoh Od Miam Chis Ta Zo Od Es V-Ma-Dea Od Pi- Bliar O Phil Rit Od Miam C-Crimi Quaada. Od. O-Michaloz Oriom Bagle Papnor I Dlugam Lonshi Od Umplif V-Ge-Gi Riglied. BABALON!

6

TheSixthInv ocation
(fromT annhauserb yA.Cr owley)

Isis art thou, and from thy life are fed
All showers and suns, all moons that wax and wane,
All stars and streams, the living and the dead,
The mystery of pleasure and of pain
Thou art the mother, thou the speaking sea
Thou art the earth, and its fertility,
Life, death, love, hatred, light, darkness return to thee
To Thee!
Hathoor am I, and to my beauty drawn
All glories of the Universe bow down,
The blossom and the mountain and the dawn
Fruits blush, and women, our creations crown
I am the priest, the sacrifice, the shrine
I the love and life of the divine
Life, death, love, hatred, light, darkness are surely mine,

Are Mine!

Venus art thou, the love and light of earth,

The wealth of kisses, the delight of tears

The barren pleasures never came to birth,

The endless infinite delight of years.

Thou art the shrine at which my long desire

Devoured me with intolerable fire.

Thou wert song, music, passion, death upon my lyre--

My lyre.

I am the Grail and I the glory now;

I am the flame and fuel of thy breast

I am the star of God upon thy brow;

*mI am the queen, enraptured and possessed,

Hide thee sweet river, welcome to thee, sea

Ocean of love that shall encompass thee

Life, death, love, hatred, light, darkness return to me--

To me!

[March2,1946E. V.continue d]

On the night of the first performance of these rituals, I pre- pared the altar and box and food, also flowers and wine. At the beginning of the rituals, I burnt the Enochian Tablet and smashed an image of Pan, a favorite possession. (About this time the roof on my guest house caught fire from a faulty chimney, and was partly destroyed.)

I proceeded with the rituals, noting a mounting tension, and the sense of a presence inexpressibly poignant and desirable. There was no other manifestation. At twelve PM I put the three ques- tions and received answers as follows:

1. How can I communicate directly with BABALON, hear her, see her, feel her, be sure that I am working aright?

Answer. "At the altar in meditation, as you know how. Also, invoke me carnally with all your passion. Thus will you feel my desire and increase my substance."

2. How can I serve best?

Answer. "Follow instructions exactly and in detail. Avoid loose interruptions. Be diligent. Do not hesitate or question, act. All depends on your time."

3. How can I be certain of the vehicle?

Answer. "Do not trouble yourself with this. It does not concern you. I will provide the vehicle, I will show you a sign, and signs. It is the now which concerns us. Keep your faith, think not overmuch."

After this an hour's meditation, and so to sleep.

[March3,1946E. V.]

The next day I slipped badly. An inmate of the house disturbed my morning meditation. I opened the door and cursed him (in the Anglo Saxon fashion). Shortly after he was taken ill, and I succumbed to a black mood. I perceived my terrible error, and apologized to him, mentally withdrawing the curse. However, the day went very badly for me. That evening the Scribe and I resumed our work. In a short time the dictation began:

"In the presence of our Lord PAN, at the feet of Our Lady BABA-LON, at the feet of Her (servants?) (changing?) we declare unto thee this message (consecrated, dedicated, never to be defiled?) (the Scribe was uncertain here) containing the rituals of the second and third days, of the welcome and preparation in the Name of Our Lady of the Night most gracious, to pure lewd and whore- some Lady BABALON. Oh thou who art mortal tremble; given it is unto thee a feat never before performed in the annals of your histories, never before accomplished successfully. Many have dared, none succeeded."

"Our Lady BABALON must descend to triumph."

"Mortality. We have not asked this of another, nor shall we ever. Even now we doubt thy faith. Is this accepted, are you willing to proceed. Answer aloud."

Answer. "I am willing."

"Then know thou art already faulty in thy delivery. These are extraneous things. The elemental was not properly released," (this was corrected) "thou wert guilty of human rage, the current of force has been disturbed. Beware, should'st thou falter again, we will sure slay thee."

"But insofar as thy working was consecrated it has succeeded. Rectify thy mortal fault and error. Consecrate all. Now receive the second and third rituals."

TheSe condRitual

[March3,1946E.   V.continue d]

"Consecrate thyself as instructor of Our Lady Incarnate."

"Take the black box, concentrate upon its emptiness for one hour, gaze into it, and thou wilt see, imprinted upon it, a shape, a sign, a sacred design, which shall be the sign delivered by Our Lady Babalon Incarnate. When thou hast finished, when thou hast recognized this pattern, construct it in wood."

"This is the sigil."

"Ten be the hour appointed. Invoke long, to music indicated." [...] (This I keep secret.) "When thou canst feel Our Lady incar- nate in thy being, take the black box and perform the consecrated rite. "Wear thou scarlet, symbolic of birth. Be sashed in black. It matters not the quality of goods. Take then the box, make then the sign."

"Paint upon it a second sign which thou knowest. If thou hast forgotten, gaze into thy crystal."

"Meditate while gazing on the qualities of an instructor. Thou shalt inscribe in Her book, for Her guidance."

"Thou art forbidden to leave thy room."

"The end of the second ritual."

At the end of this dictation, the Scribe showed signs of exhaus- tion. He rested awhile, then we continued:

TheThir dRitual

[March31946E. V.continue d]

"Begin four hours prior to dawn."

"A period of eradication of all inimical influences. Complete perfection. Wear black. Cut from thy breast the red star. Renew the blood. Lay out a white sheet. Place upon it blood of birth, since She is born of thy flesh, and by thy mortal power upon earth."

"Thou shalt recognize by the sign. BABALON is born! It is new birth, all things are changed, the signs, the symbols, the every- thing!"

"Thou shalt compass with the aid of the muse suitable invocation of the birth of BABALON, and this thou shalt deliver to the flames which now burn too."

"Now thou shalt flame the third, chanting the invocation. She is born in the third flame."

"In verse seven verses of seven lines, seven magick words. Stand and chant seven times. Envision thyself as a cloaked radiance desirable to the Goddess, beloved. Envision Her approaching thee. Embrace Her, cover Her with kisses. Think upon the lewd lascivi- ous things thou couldst do. All is good to BABALON. ALL.

"Then rest, meditating on this:"

"Thou as a man and as a god hast strewn about the earth and in the heavens many loves, these recall, concentrate, consecrate each woman thou hast raped. Remember her, think upon her, move her into BABALON, bring her into BABALON, each, one by one until the flame of lust is high."

"Then compose a verse of undetermined lines on this, to BABALON. This verse shall be used in worship when she appears."

"Then meditate upon thy desire, think upon Her, and, touching naught, chant these verses. Recall each lascivious moment, each lustfull day, all set them into the astral body, touching naught."

"Preserve the material basis."

(Question: "In the box?" Answer: "Yes.")

"The lust is hers, the passion yours. Consider thou the Beast raping."

"Leave thy casual loves--all belongs to BABALON, thy lust is BABALON's. She is with thee three days. The sign is hers, secret, and no man knows its correspondence. Guard!"

The next section contains a prophecy which I shall not write here.

There follows the indicated invoking poem.

The Birth of Babalon

What is the tumult among the stars
that have shone so still till now?
What are the furrows of pain and wrath
upon the immortal brow?
Why is the face of God turned grey
and his angels all grown white?
What is the terrible ruby star
that burns down the crimson night?
What is the beauty that flames so bright
athwart the awful dawn?
She has taken flesh, she is come to judge
the thrones ye rule upon.

Quail ye kings for an end is come
in the birth of BABALON.

I have walked three dreadful nights away
in halls beyond despair,
I have given marrow and tears and sweat
and blood to make her fair.

I have lain my love and smashed my heart
and filled her cup with blood,
That blood might flow from the loins of woe
to the cup of brotherhood.

The cities reel in the shout of steel
where the sword of war is drawn.
Sing ye saints for the day is come
in the birth of BABALON.

Now God has called for his judgement book
and seen his name therein
And the grace of God and the guilt of God
have spelt it out as sin

His bloody priests have clutched his robes
and stained his linen gown
And his victims swarm from his broken hell
to drag his kingdom down.

O popes and kings and the little gods
are sick and sad and wan
To see the crimson star that bursts
like blood upon the dawn
While trumpets sound and stars rejoice
at the birth of BABALON.

BABALON is too beautiful
for sight of mortal eyes
She has hidden her loveliness away
in lonely midnight skies,
She has clothed her beauty in robes of sin
and pledged her heart to swine
And loving and giving all she has
brewed for saints immortal wine.

But now the darkness is riven through
and the robes of sin are gone,
And naked she stands as a terrible blade
and a flame and a splendid song
Naked in radiant mortal flesh
at the Birth of BABALON.

She is come new born as a mortal maid
forgetting her high estate,
She has opened her arms to pain and death
and dared the doom of fate,
And death and hell are at her back,
but her eyes are bright with life,
Her heart is high and her sword is strong
to meet the deadly strife,
Her voice is sure as the judgement trump
to crack the house of wrong,
Though walls are high and stone is hard
and the rule of hell was long
The gates shall fall and the irons break
in the Birth of BABALON.

Her mouth is red and her breasts are fair
and her loins are full of fire,
And her lust is strong as a man is strong
in the heat of her desire,
And her whoredom is holy as virtue is foul
beneath the holy sky,
And her kisses will wanton the world away
in passion that shall not die.
Ye shall laugh and love and follow her dance
when the wrath of God is gone
And dream no more of hell and hate
in the Birth of BABALON.

THEBOOKOFANTICHRIST

TheBlackPilgrimag e

Now it came to pass even as BABALON told me, for after receving Her Book I fell away from Magick, and put away Her Book and all pertaining thereto. And I was stripped of my fortune (the sum of about $50,000) and my house, and all I Possessed.

Then for a period of two years I worked in the world, recouping my fortune somewhat. But that was also taken from me, and my reputation, and my good name in my worldly work, that was in science.

And on the 31st of October, 1948, BABALON called on me again, and I began the last work, that was the work of the wand. And I worked for 17 days, until BABALON called me in a dream, and instructed me on an astral working. Then I reconstructed the temple, and began the Black Pilgrimage, as She instructed.

And I went into the sunset with Her sign, and into the night past accursed and desolate places and cyclopean ruins, and so came at last to the City of Chorazin. And there a great tower of Black Basalt was raised, that was part of a castle whose further bat- tlements reeled over the gulf of stars. And upon the tower was this sign

And one heavily robed and veiled showed me the sign, and told me to look, and hehold, I saw flash below me four past lives wherein I had failed in my object. And I beheld the life of Simon Magus, preaching the Whore Helena as the Sophia, and I saw that my failure was in Hubris, the pride of the spirit. And I saw my life as Giles de Retz, wherein I attempted to raise Jehanne Darc to be Queen of the Witchcraft, and failed through her stupidity, and again my pride. And I saw myself in Francis Hepburne, Earl Both- well, manipulating

Gellis Duncan, that was an unworthy instru- ment. And again as Count Cagliostro, failing because I failed to comprehend the nature of women in my Seraphina. And I was shown myself as a boy of 13 in this life, invoking Satan and showing cowardice when He appeared. And I was asked: "Will you fail again?" and I replied "I will not fail." (For I had given all my blood to BABALON, and it was not I that spoke.)

And thereafter I was taken within and saluted the Prince of that place, and thereafter things were done to me of which I may not write, and they told me, "It is not certain that you will sur- vive, but if you survive you will attain your true will, and manifest the Antichrist.

And thereafter I returned and swore the Oath of the Abyss, having only the choice between madness, suicide, and that oath. But the Oath in no wise ameliorated that terror, and I continued in the madness and horror of the abyss for a season. But of this no more. But having passed the ordeal of 40 days I took the oath of a Magister Templi, even the Oath of Antichrist before Frater 132, the Unknown God.

And thus was I Antichrist loosed in the world; and to this I am pledged, that the work of the Beast 666 shall be fulfilled, and the way for the coming of BABALON be made open and I shall not cease or rest until these things are accomplished. And to this end I have issued this my Manifesto.

TheManifestooftheAntichrist

Do what thou wilt shall be the whole of the Law.

I, BELARION, ANTICHRIST, in the year 1949 of the rule of the Black Brotherhood called Christianity, do make my Manifesto to all men. And I, THE ANTICHRIST, come among you, saying:

An end to the pretence, and lying hypocrisy of Christianity.

An end to the servile virtues, and superstitious restrictions.

An end to the slave morality.

An end to prudery and shame, to guild and sin, for these are of the only evil the sun, that is fear.

An end to all authority that is not based on courage and manhood, to the authority of lying priests, conniving judges, blackmailing police, and

An end to the servile flattery and cajolery of mods, the corona- tions of mediocraties, the ascension of dolts.

An end to restriction and inhibition, for I, THE ANTICHRIST, am come among you preaching the Word of the BEAST 666, which is, "There is no law beond Do what thou wilt."

And I, BELARION, ANTICHRIST, do lift up my voice and prophecy, and I say:

I shall bring all men to the law of the BEAST 666, and in His law I shall conquer the world.

And within seven years of this time, BABALON, THE SCARLET WOMAN HILARION will manifest among ye, and bring this my work to its fruition.

An end to consciption, compulsion, regimentation, and the tyranny of false laws.

And within nine years a nation shall accept the Law of the BEAST 666 in my name, and that nation will be the first nation of earth.

And all who accept me the ANTICHRIST and the law of the BEAST 666, shall be accursed and their joy shall be a thousandfold greater than the false joys of the false saints.

And in my name BELARION shall they work miracles, and confound our enemies, and none shall stand before us.

Therefore I, THE ANTICHRIST call upon all the Chosen and elect and upon all men, come forth now in the name of Liberty, that we may end for ever the tyranny of the Black Brotherhood.

Witness my hand and seal on this [...] day of [...] 1949, that is the year of BABALON 4066.

Love is the law, love under will.

Belarion, Antichrist

Analysis By A Master Of The Temple

OftheCriticalNo desintheExp erienceofhisMaterialV ehicle

"I shall regard all phenomena as the particular dealing of God with my soul."

I.Birth

Oct. 2, 1914, Los Angeles, in , rising in midheaven, in favorable conjunc., at apehelion. I chose this constellation in order that you might have an innate sense of balance and ultimate justice, responsive and attractive nature, a bountiful environment and sense of royalty and largesse, strength, courage and power combined with cunning and intelligence. Saturn was bound in order that you might easily formulate a lower will which would have satisfied and overwhelmed you with its spectacular success.

Your father separated from your mother in order that you might grow up with a hatred of authority and a spirit of revolution necessary to my work. The Oedipus complex was needed to formulate the love of witchcraft which would lead you into magick, with the influence of your grandfather active to prevent too complete an identification with your mother.

II.Childho od

Your isolation as a child developed the necessary background of literature and scholarship; and the unfortunate experiences with other children the requisite contempt for the crowd and for the group mores. You will note that these factors developed the needful hatred for christianity (without implanting a christian guilt sense) at an extremely early age.

III.A dolescence

Early adolescence continued the development of the necessary combinations. The awakening interest in chemistry and science prepared the counterbalance for the coming magical awakening, the means of obtaining prestige and livelihood in the formative period, and the scientific method necessary for my manifestation. The magical fiasco at the age of 16 was needful to keep you away from magick until you were sufficiently matured.

IV.Y outh

The loss of family fortune developed your sense of self reliance at a critical period, the contact with reality at this time was essential. Your early marriage with Helen served to break your family ties and effect a transference to her, away from a danger- ous attachment to your mother. The experience at Halifax and Cal Tech served to strengthen your self reliance, scientific method and material powers. The influence of Tom Rose at this period, as that of Ed. Forman in adolescence, was essential in developing the male center.

V.LaterY outh

The house on Terrace Drive, Music, Lynn, Curtis, and Gloria, and the increasing restlessness were, of course, all preparations for the meeting with A A and O.T.O. The alternate repulsion and attraction you felt the first year after meeting Fra. 132 were caused by a subconscious resistance against the ordeals ahead. Had you had these experiences before, without such resistance, you would have become hopelessly unbalanced. Betty served to effect a transference from Helen at a critical period. Had this not occurred your repressed homosexual component could have caused a serious disorder.

Your passion for Betty also gave you the magical force needed at the time, and the act of adultery tinged with incest, served as your magical confirmation in the Law of Thelema.

At this time the O.T.O. was an excellent training school for adepts, but hardly an appropriate Order for the manifestation of Thelema. Therefore, in spite of your motto you were not able to formulate your Will. The experience with the O.T.O. and Aerijet were needed to dispel your romanticism, self-deception, and reliance on others. Betty was one link in the process designed to tear you away from the now unneeded Oedipus complex, the overval- uation of women and romantic love. Since this was unconscious, the next step was to bring it into consciousness, and there to destroy it.

VI.EarlyMaturity

The final experience with Hubbard and Betty, and the O.T.O. was necessary to overcome your false and infantile reliance on oth- ers, although this was only partially accomplished at the time. The invocation of Babalon served to exteriorize the Oedipus complex; at the same time, because of the forces involved it produced extraordinary magical effects. However, this operation is accomplished and closed--you should have nothing more to do with it--nor even think of it, until Her manifestation is re- vealed, and proved beyond the shadow of a doubt. Even then, you must be circumspect--although I hope to take complete charge before then.

Candy appeared in answer to your call, in order to wean you from wet nursing. She has demonstrated the nature of woman to you in such unequivocal terms that you should have no further room for illusion on the subject.

The suspension and inquisition was my opportunity--one of the final links in the chain. At this time you were enabled to pre- pare your thesis, formulate your Will, and take the Oath of the Abyss, thus making it possible (although only partially) to manifest. The exit of Candy prepares for the final stage of your initial preparation.

VII.Conclusions

The numerous rituals you have performed have resulted in a well developed body of light. The ordeals have purged most of the emotional and mental garbage--your only real dangers are, and have ever been, sentimentality, weakness, and procrastination.

It is interesting to note that the first weapon you formulated was the Lamp of the Spirit, in the invocation to Pan (although the Sword was prefigured). Next the Sword in the Horus ritual, as was appropriate to your intellectual development at that time.

Then the Cup out of the wine of your emotional life--the disk out of material failure. The Sword remains to be manifested.

You will note that it has been impossible to truly formulate your Will with any of these weapons--naturally--that is only possible with the wand. On the other hand, if you had done so previously, you would have been unbalanced by the lack of initiated prepara- tion. It is a right and natural procedure; the True Will cannot be truly formulated until you are initiate in all the other planes, and it is well to make no pretense of doing so. Until that point all you can known of the true will is the aspiration to the next step--towards further experience. That is the glory of the Law of Thelema--DO!

The physical and emotional stresses you feel at present are a result of the pull of the Abyss--your present poetry is indica- tive. Naturally you find no power in any spell, no comfort in any ritual, no hope in any action. You are cut off by your own oath. Nor can I or any other aid you at this time. There is only manhood, only will, only the vector of your own tendencies, developed through the aeons of the past. I do not say how long the state will last, or what the outcome may be.

However, I can formulate some rules which may serve to guide you.

VIII.Instr uctions

A. Works of the Wand--of the Will alone avail in this state. No other weapon should be used, no other ritual save the hymn to the Unnamed One in the Anthem of the Mass.

B. You should be meticulous in all observations pertaining to the Will, even the most petty. Fulfill all obligations and promises, undertake nothing which you cannot fulfill, be prompt in the discharge of each responsibility.

C. Be neat in your personal and domestic habits, indicate your selfrespect to yourself.

D. Do not become unduly involved with any person, and practice all your hard-earned wisdom in your relations with women.

E. Set up your personal affairs in business order. Keep your accounts current and your papers neatly filed.

F. Finish your poetry for publication. Finish the synthesis of the Tarot and start work on the preparation of the lessons of class instruction from your book.

G. Pay no attention to any phenomena whatsoever, and continue in a sober and responsible way of life under all circumstances.

Not magical! For you nothing is more magical. Only thus can the curse of Saturn be overcome. I see you hate this way. But it is an ultimate time--it is you that have taken the oath. The choice is me or Choronzon.

I await you in the City of the Pyramids.

Belarion

8 = 3

Table des matières

The Book Of Babalon   5
The Book Of Antichrist   28
Analysis By A Master Of The Temple   32